# FROM SOLID GOLD TO BROKEN CLAY

A CLEAR AND PRESENT TRUTH MESSAGE

**Rapid Movements Publishing**
Hampton, GA 30228

Copyright © 2021 by Tory St.Cyr

Printed in the United States of America
All Rights Reserved

Published by Rapid Movements Publishing
Hampton, GA 30228


Other books by Tory St.Cyr may be purchased at
www.clearandpresenttruth.com

The author assumes full responsibility for the accuracy of all facts and quotations, as cited in this book.

ISBN: 978-1-7366073-3-6


Pictures and illustrations used by permission of Freepik.com

This book is dedicated to those of us who are still running this Christian race.

# Contents

*Preface* ............................................................................ 9

***MORE THAN AN IMAGE*** .................................................... 11

***THE GOLDEN PHASE*** ...................................................... 25

***THE SILVER PHASE*** ........................................................ 33

***THE BRASS PHASE*** ........................................................ 39

***THE IRON PHASE*** .......................................................... 47

***THE IRON AND CLAY PHASE*** ........................................... 55

***GETTING BACK TO GOLD*** ............................................... 67

## Preface

The message contained in this book is a sermon I preached for Youth Day. The purpose of this message was twofold: 1) Our youth need to understand prophecy and see that the Word of God is true. 2) I wanted the youth to understand that there are nuggets of truth all throughout the Scriptures. One of these nuggets that I discovered was hidden within the image that Nebuchadnezzar saw in his dream.

Primarily, Nebuchadnezzar's image represents a number of kingdoms that were to rule the world. However, I revealed to the youth that there is a secondary application that personally relates to each and every individual—including you.

You are about to see that the image Nebuchadnezzar saw in his dream is also a blueprint used by Satan. However, even though Satan has a blueprint, you are about to discover that God has one too.

# Chapter 1

# MORE THAN AN IMAGE

*And in the second year of the reign of Nebuchadnezzar Nebuchadnezzar dreamed dreams, wherewith his spirit was troubled, and his sleep brake from him. Daniel 2:1*

I can remember growing up in the church as a young adolescent. I can also recall a number of programs, events, and activities that our church had for the youth. There was Sabbath School, Youth Ministries, socials, and an array of activities geared towards young people. However, the one event I always anticipated was children's story time. For those of you who are unfamiliar with the term, this was the time in the church service when the young kids would go to the front of the church and listen to a short story given by a church member. I can recall sitting on the hard green carpet with my legs crossed and my attention hanging on every word of the storyteller. The narrations given by these individuals always made me feel as if I were right in the midst of the story.

One of my favorite stories told during children's story was the account of Nebuchadnezzar's dream. I could envision the king waking from his sleep. I could see his confusion and astonishment, knowing he had an important dream but unable to recall it. I put myself in the action as he interrogated his wise men to no satisfaction. My heart raced as Daniel prayed all night for his life and the lives of his friends. I could feel the tension as Daniel approached King Nebuchadnezzar's throne. And I felt the relief as Daniel revealed the dream and the interpretation to the king.

As a young child, I hadn't fully grasped the profoundness of Nebuchadnezzar's dream. I didn't understand that the king's dream was still relevant. It wasn't until I got older that I began to understand the magnitude of this dream. God showed the king that his kingdom was part of a series of nations that would rule the world.

The head of gold represented Babylon. However, the King of Babylon was told that his kingdom would not last forever. Babylon would one day fall! The question we need to answer is what was the main reason behind the downfall of Nebuchadnezzar's Empire?

One of the main contributors to the downfall of the Babylonian Empire was clearly seen in the character of the Babylonian king. As a matter of fact, this character flaw was so prevalent in Nebuchadnezzar that God punished the king for seven years. Notice how the Book of Daniel presents Nebuchadnezzar's biggest character flaw:

> "Is not this great Babylon, that I have built for the house of the kingdom by the might of my power, and for the honour of my majesty?" Daniel 4:30

From this text we can see that King Nebuchadnezzar had a problem with pride. The next chapter of Daniel would reveal that this pride "apple" didn't fall too far from the family tree as his grandson, Belshazzar, had this same issue. Notice Daniel's final words to the last Babylonian ruler:

> "...And thou his son, O Belshazzar, hast not humbled thine heart, though thou knewest all this; But hast lifted up thyself against the Lord of heaven..." Daniel 5:22-23

From these Scripture references, we can see that Babylon's downfall was a result of pride.

The prophecy then revealed that another kingdom would arise after Babylon's demise. The chest and arms of silver were none other than the Medo-Persian Empire.

This powerful empire controlled the known world. But just as silver holds less value than gold, Medo-Persia would never be as glorious as its predecessor, Babylon.

Regarding the nation represented by the arms and chest of silver, Daniel 11:2 says, "*there shall stand up yet three kings in Persia; and the fourth shall be far richer than they all: and by his strength through his riches he shall stir up all against the realm of Grecia.*" Hidden within this text is the downfall of the Persian Empire. History reveals that Greece consisted of several city-states. However, they were all divided and ruled locally. The fourth king after Darius the Mede was known as Xerxes. This Persian king's expensive campaign against the Grecian city-states compelled the divided territories to combine forces against the world-ruling power. Losing the battles of Salamis and Plataea, it appears the Persians may have underestimated the Greek alliance. Suffering small losses to the Greeks revealed the superiority of the brass nation. However, the rulers in Persia didn't realize that these small losses foreshadowed a major defeat and ultimately the downfall of the Persian Empire.

Rising to power as Persia declined, Alexander the Great became the ruler of the known world. Conquering the world faster than any of his predecessors, Alexander the Great's title was no exaggeration. Unfortunately for him, his greatness was short-lived as he died suddenly at the height of his power.

The nation of brass reeled into mass confusion as his friends, family, and political inner circle, all fought for control of the Empire. As the nation fell into civil war, the well-being of the Empire was no longer a priority.

Because the divided Greek rulers were so consumed with their individual territories, they failed to see a threat rising from the west—and this would prove to be their downfall.

Coming from the west, the Roman Empire would end up conquering the divided Grecian territories. Rome, represented by the legs of iron, brought the world to its knees. Rising from its humble beginnings as a small settlement, the fourth kingdom slowly increased with power and might to become one of the world's most powerful and influential nations.

Along with this power and influence came an exponential increase in territory. Rome had the largest territory of all its predecessors, but with this large territory came an abundance of problems.

Due to the size of the Roman Empire, it was unable to defend all its borders. This inability to defend its borders proved to be the downfall of the Empire. In the fifth century, scores of Barbarian tribes infiltrated Rome from the north resulting in the fall of the western half of the empire.

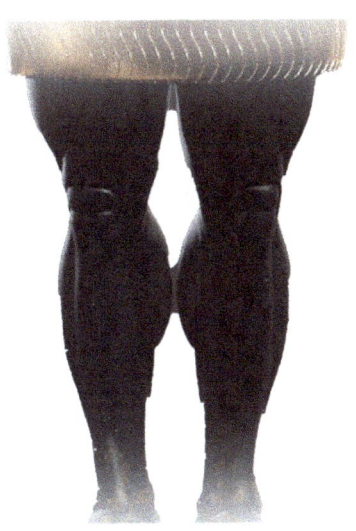

As the Western Roman Empire saw its nation ransacked by the invading Barbarian tribes, the emperor declared the Bishop of Rome as the head of the Christian Church. This declaration resulted in a man obtaining civil authority in addition to the religious authority he already possessed. Church and State combined, and thus the Papacy was established.

Symbolized by the feet and toes of iron and clay, Papal Rome was given authority for 1260 years. Beginning in 538 AD and ending 1798 AD, the Papacy's authority came to an end after Pope Pius VI was captured by the French.

The reason for the Papacy's downfall is a direct result of the war it waged against the Bible. By giving their priest and popes the power to forgive sins, changing the Sabbath, elevating Mary, and embracing a host of other false teachings, Papal Rome declared war on the Word of God.

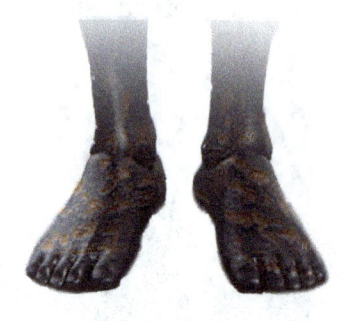

Even though the Papacy fell, these false teachings have and will continue until the image is destroyed by the stone.

The dream given to Nebuchadnezzar is still applicable to this day. History confirms the accuracy of Daniel's prophecy as we are currently living during the time of the ten toes of iron and clay. The final phase reveals the image being broken to pieces by a stone cut out of a mountain.

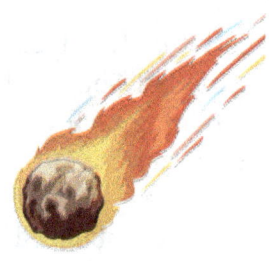

While the intent of this prophecy was clearly given to show Nebuchadnezzar the future of the world, I have recently began understanding that Nebuchadnezzar's image also reveals another important truth. This truth concerns every person regardless of their age, gender, or color. What led me to this discovery was the following statement written by Ellen White:

> "The image revealed to Nebuchadnezzar, while representing the deterioration of the kingdoms of the earth in power and glory, also fitly represents the deterioration of religion and morality among the people of these kingdoms. As nations forget God, in like proportion they become weak morally." *Ellen White, The Youth Instructor, September 22, 1903.*

As I contemplated the words of Ellen White, I began to see that there was more to Nebuchadnezzar's image than I initially understood. The image also represents the deterioration of religion and morality among the people. This truth became more relevant when I read this quote from the Book of Lamentations:

> "How the gold has lost its luster,

the fine gold become dull! The sacred gems are scattered at every street corner. How the precious children of Zion, once worth their weight in gold, are now considered as pots of clay, the work of a potter's hands!" Lamentations 4:1-2 NIV

Do you see it? God once considered the Children of Zion as gold, but because of their disobedience, he relegated their worth to pots of clay. In other words, God had high expectations for his people, but they responded to these high expectations with low standards. This reminds me of the time I thought my baseball card collection would make me a wealthy teenager. From my early adolescent years, I had been holding a stack of baseball cards in my possession. Even though I didn't recognize any of the players, I assumed that one day they would make me a rich kid.

My best friend's older brother overheard me talking about my baseball card collection and offered to "appraise" my stack. Since he was a self-proclaimed baseball card expert, I agreed that he would have the privilege of watching me become an instant millionaire in person.

As we sat in my front yard that Sunday afternoon, he attentively watched as I handed him a sandwich bag containing a stack of about 50 baseball cards.

For the next 5 minutes, I watched as he examined each card. I stood by, watching him with bated breath as he flipped each card around, felt their edges, and talked under his breath.

After what seemed like a lifetime, he handed the stack of cards back to me. He paused and smiled. Was he happy at my seven-figure breakthrough? He seemed almost at a loss of words.

Finally, he broke the silence to inform me that in order for a baseball card to be worth serious money, three things had to be true: 1) The card should be a rookie baseball card. 2) The player had to be historically great. 3) The card had to be in near perfect condition.

After revealing the criteria, he informed me that my cards missed all three of the benchmarks: None of the cards were rookies, none of the players were great, and none of the cards were in good condition (The sandwich bag probably told you all you needed to know about their condition). He topped this conversation off by revealing to me that a baseball card dealer might give me a dollar to take the cards off my hands. It was then that I understood why he smiled.

I was crushed. My dream of being a wealthy

teenager became null and void in the blink of an eye. What I thought was priceless, was in fact, worthless.

Even though that example is on a much smaller scale, we must understand that God experienced a similar disappointment with the Children of Israel. Just as I had hoped my cards would be valuable, God had hoped His people could be compared to gold. However, just as I was saddened at the fact my cards were worthless, God was disappointed to know His people were only worth the value of clay. Do you see it? What God hoped would be solid gold ended up as pots of clay! The question is, how could the people who were supposed to be gold end up becoming pots of clay? The answer is found in Daniel 2.

Ladies and gentlemen, the image of Daniel 2 is more than an image of the world's empires. Hidden within this image is a blueprint...a system used by Satan to cause a solid gold Christian to become a broken clay sinner.

In the next few pages, you are going to see this image in a whole new light. However, before we delve into the details of the image, it is imperative that you remember the reason each nation fell from its place on the world's stage:

- **Babylon** – Pride
- **Medo-Persia** – Underestimated the enemy; Was blind to the small losses

that foreshadowed a major defeat.
- **Greece** – Individual territories were prioritized over the Empire.
- **Rome** – Infiltrated due to its inability to protect its borders.
- **Papal Rome** - Declared war against the Bible.

Now that we've recalled the reason for each empire's downfall, you must understand that each kingdom also represents a phase in our relationship with Christ. Gold represents someone who has fully surrendered to Christ, while broken clay represents someone who is a slave to sin.

It may not be apparent at the moment, but you will also discover that the way each of these nations fell in the real world matches the way Satan causes our downfall in the spiritual world.

## 24 • FROM SOLID GOLD TO BROKEN CLAY

# Chapter 2

# **THE GOLDEN PHASE**

As the golden head was the most precious metal of the image, Christians in the golden phase are the most sincere followers of Christ.

As I contemplated the meaning of the golden phase of Christianity, a quote from the Bible came to mind:

> "Enter ye in at the strait gate: for wide is the gate, and broad is the way, that leadeth to destruction, and **many** there

> be which go in thereat: Because strait is the gate, and narrow is the way, which leadeth unto life, and **few** there be that find it." Matthew 7:13-14

This scripture also reminded me of a quote I read from one of Ellen White's books:

> "It is a solemn statement that I make to the church, that not one in twenty whose names are registered upon the church books are prepared to close their earthly history, and would be as verily without God and without hope in the world as the common sinner." *Christian Service, p 41*

Reading this statement as a youth, I found myself counting the members of my church, trying to determine who were the "one in twenty" of my local congregation. Interestingly, I would always include myself as a part of the one in twenty, but that's another story.

Here, Ellen White is simply making the point that most people who consider themselves to be followers of Christ aren't truly following Him. Yes, our names are listed as members of the church, and we are known by all our friends and family to be Christian, but that's really as far as it goes. In other words, most of us who consider ourselves followers of Christ are not in the golden phase of Christianity.

Jesus revealed what a Christian in the golden phase is like when he addressed a lawyer's question about the greatest commandment. Notice His response:

> "Thou shalt love the Lord thy God with all thy heart, and with all thy soul, and with all thy mind. This is the first and great commandment. And the second is like unto it, Thou shalt love thy neighbour as thyself." Matthew 22:37-39

Here, we can see that a true believer is one who loves God and loves his fellow man. Love is at the heart of being a true Christian because our motivation for following Jesus should not be out of fear or because we don't want to be lost. Our willingness to follow Jesus must be based on a true deep love for God and for humanity.

Some church members live only to make others believe they are Christians; however, believers in the golden phase are just as faithful behind closed doors as they are on stage in front of a congregation.

Believers who are in the golden phase of Christianity walk their talk. They are in constant prayer and study. They trust in the Lord with all their heart, and they truly live to please Him. They guard the avenues of their souls by not listening to anything that would offend Christ. They are not watching shows that would prove detrimental to their soul-salvation. They are not entering into places that would hinder the Holy Spirit from communicating with them. While they are still sinners, they are perfect because they have surrendered their wills to Christ.

Christians in this stage are not, as I call it, hourly-based believers; they are salary-based believers. Allow me to explain:

One of my first jobs was doing phone support for a Fortune 500 company. When I arrived at work, I did what was required of me and nothing more. When the clock struck 5:30 pm, I got up from my desk and walked out of the building. Once I clocked out, I did not talk about work, nor did I think about work. The company paid me to work by the hour, and once those hours were over, so was my interest in all work-related matters.

However, my manager was salary-based. Her work was not based upon a certain set of hours. She was so dedicated to the job that she woke up thinking about work. She would discuss job functions during her lunch hour. She would often take calls once she got home from the office, and even on her vacations, she would call to make sure the business was running smoothly.

While the world can consist of hourly-based employees who work hard around the clock and salary-based employees who do absolutely nothing, the example I have given should help you understand the tendencies of a salary-based Christian.

A Christian in the golden stage of their walk does not "clock out" of Christianity. They are focused on Jesus before they go to sleep and after they wake up. They are not followers of Christ only during the church "working" hours. They are full-time Christians. If I were asked to sum up a gold-stage Christian using one word, I would say that they are converted. However, you must understand that there is an "Achilles' heel" for believers in the golden phase.

## The Downfall of the Gold Phase

Believers in the golden phase are not immune to temptation. As Satan studied the image, he made a startling discovery: The same way golden Babylon fell in the real world, is the same way a gold-level Christian falls in the spiritual world.

Satan realized the one thing that believers in the golden stage can be susceptible to is pride. Just as King Nebuchadnezzar started believing that his accomplishments were by his own hands, Christians in the gold phase can be deceived into believing that they are the source of their own righteousness. The Bible is clear on the result of this type of pride:

> "Pride comes before destruction, and an arrogant spirit before a fall." Proverbs 16:18 CSB

If Believers in the golden phase are not watching, they will begin to believe that they are the reason souls are being saved. They will start to count how many Bible studies they've given; they will start to believe their voice and their talents are the only thing keeping the church going and may even be tempted to think that God cannot complete the gospel work without them. Whenever these prideful thoughts come into the minds of these believers, they must reject them at once. Why? The Bible does not mince words.

> "Wherefore let him that thinketh he standeth take heed lest he fall."
> 1Corinthians 10:12

Christians in the golden phase must understand that the longer they entertain these thoughts, the easier it becomes to fall from the golden phase and transition to the silver phase of Christianity.

# FROM SOLID GOLD TO BROKEN CLAY

# Chapter 3

# **THE SILVER PHASE**

Silver-phase Christians are a little more common among church members. What makes the silver phase so dangerous is that these individuals look and act just like individuals in the golden stage. As a matter of fact, it is almost impossible to tell the difference. They dress modestly. Their conversation is pure. All indications would have you believe that they have surrendered all to Christ. What separates the silver stage from the golden stage is really a matter of character. Individuals who make up the silver phase are simply gold-phase Christians with one character flaw. What makes a silver-phase Christian so hard to identify is the fact that their Christian qualities are so dominant that most people simply overlook their spiritual flaws.

In case you are curious, here are a few examples of character flaws found in silver-phase Christians:

- They follow the health laws, but they will act as if they've been eating tiger meat when under stressful situations.
- They will dress modestly but still crave attention.
- They are well versed in the Bible, but their motive is to prove they are smarter than everyone else.
- They'll wait on the Lord but have no patience for others.
- They can often be critical of people struggling with issues that they themselves had no problems overcoming.
- They excel at major issues but fail at minor issues.

Hopefully by now, you get the picture.

A Christian that's in the silver stage of their walk exhibits the Fruit of the Spirit, but there are some brown spots on that fruit. Notice, I didn't say they lacked the fruit. An inspection will reveal they have the Fruit of the Spirit; however, that fruit is a bit overripe.

Oftentimes, when a believer in the silver phase is caught in sin, you will hear people say things like, "I thought Sister So-and-So was spiritual; can you believe what she did? Or you will hear people say things like this: I thought Brother So-and-So was a nice person. Did you see how he treated me after we had a disagreement in Bible study?

This sums up a silver-stage Christian. They are gold-stage Christians with one major character flaw. Most aren't aware of this character flaw because it only rears its ugly head in pressurized moments. These pressurized moments are rarely seen because most encounters with silver-stage Christians are under the best of circumstance (i.e., Bible study, prayer meeting, and church potlucks).

It is true that many Christians will experience a spiritual struggle; however, what sets the silver-stage Christian apart from the rest is that they have the same problem that the Persian Empire had—they overestimate themselves and underestimate the enemy.

## The Downfall of the Silver Phase

Because most silver-phase Christians believe

they are in the gold stage, they are apt to overestimate themselves while underestimating the enemy.

Just like the Persians remained confident despite losing multiple battles to the Greek alliance, believers in the silver phase are often oblivious that they are taking losses on the spiritual battlefield. They are preoccupied and don't realize they are not in prayer as often as they used to be.  They don't see that they are less diligent about studying the Scriptures. These are considered minor setbacks, but those in the silver stage don't realize that these "minor" setbacks foreshadow a major backslide.

Believers in the silver phase begin sliding down the image with a misspoken word here or slip-up there. Silver-stage Christians don't realize that the same issues they were previously victorious over are now becoming areas of concern. Movies they never used to watch are now becoming part of their nightly routine. They'll begin listening to a song or two that they hadn't listened to in years. They are going down a spiritual slide, but the fall is so slow they are not able to recognize it.

Luke 11:21-22 says, "*When a strong man armed keepeth his palace, his goods are in peace: But when a stronger than he shall come upon him, and overcome him, he taketh from him all his armour wherein he trusted, and divideth his spoils.*" This is how a silver-stage Christian falls—they stop relying on the strength of Christ, which results in them being overpowered by the enemy. However, the silver-phase Christian must be careful. The more they rely on self, the further they will begin to slide down the spectrum of the image. They must understand that they are not far from brass.

# Chapter 4

# **THE BRASS PHASE**

Of all the different phases of Christianity, the brass phase is the largest. Not only is brass the largest in population, but its range is also very broad. Whether you realize it, most Christians you meet will be part of the brass stage. Due to the vastness of its range, you will discover that some brass Christians are closer to silver, while other brass Christians are closer to iron. Regardless of where a brass-level Christian is within the range, he or she must understand that they are still a brass-level Christian.

You may be wondering why the brass phase is the most popular phase of the image. The answer to this question becomes self-evident once you contemplate the location of the belly and thighs of brass. What do I mean? The belly and thighs of brass are at the center of the image. The brass is not too expensive like silver or gold, but it's not too cheap like clay. It's right in the middle of the pack. Christians in the brass phase are essentially comfortable. They are not low enough to feel that they are lost, but they are not too high to feel that they must sacrifice their way of life. In essence, they don't want to be cold or hot—they are comfortable being lukewarm.

The Bible is clear about being a lukewarm Christian. Revelation 3:15-16 says, "*I know thy works, that thou art neither cold nor hot: I would thou wert cold or hot. So then because thou art lukewarm, and neither cold nor hot, I will spue thee out of my mouth.*"

The Church of Laodicea represents the Christian in the brass stage. This lukewarm state manifests itself in a variety of ways. Here are a few:

# THE BRASS PHASE • 41

- Christians in the brass phase love church, but they also love the world.
- Brass-level Christians will know the Word of God, but they will also know the lyrics to the most recent rap song.
- Brass-level Christians typically want to work in the church but will only accept roles that allow them to still feel comfortable living in sin.
- Christians in the brass know they need a spiritual makeover, but they lack the motivation to change.
- Brass-level Christians are often content with small spiritual victories because these small victories make them feel that they are winning the spiritual battle.

Just like believers in the gold phase are considered salary-based, Christians in the brass phase are considered hourly-based. Brass-level Christians are on a spiritual clock. Many of them do great work during "church hours." They may even appear as gold-level Christians during "high time," however, once these believers "clock out," their brass-ness will become evident. Spiritual matters will no longer be discussed, Bible study will no longer be desired, and prayer will essentially become nonexistent.

What you must understand about the believers who make up the brass stage is that they are subconsciously trying to be saved while doing the bare minimum. When I think of the bare minimum, I am forced to think of my time in high school. The bare minimum was my mantra. I studied just enough not to fail my classes. I often arrived late to school but would leave as soon as I heard the bell. Study time was almost nonexistent, and extra credit was simply too extra for me to do it. And even though I did get through high school with bare minimum effort, brass-level Christians must understand this will not work with their soul salvation.

In Matthew 25, the story is told of a man who traveled to a far country. He called his servants and gave all three of them a set amount of money with the expectation that they would invest that money and make a profit. However, after some time passed, the man returned to discover only two of his three servants made profits by investing what was given to them. The third servant informed his master that he made zero in profits. Thinking that he had a valid reason, the servant said,

> "I was afraid I would lose your money, so I hid it in the earth. Look, here is your money back." Matthew 25:25 (NLT)

The third servant in this story was expected to increase what his master had given him; instead, he decided to return what he was given. In essence, the servant attempted to get away with doing the bare minimum and still satisfy his master's request. The story reveals that the master was not happy about the servant's results and *cast the unprofitable servant into outer darkness* where there was *weeping and gnashing of teeth* (Matthew 25:30).

Believers who make up the brass stage must understand that bare-minimum religion does not work in the end. They may satisfy the requirements of the other church members, but God requires His people to have works along with their faith.

Unfortunately, the degradation of morality is still a possibility, and thus Satan's method to cause a brass-level Christian to fall is revealed in the fall of the Greek Empire.

## The Downfall of the Brass Phase

The fall of Greece reveals how Satan attacks believers in the brass phase. If you recall, Greece broke into civil war after Alexander the Great died. This civil war resulted in a fractured empire. The Greek Empire now consisted of various rulers who only cared about their own territories. The north no longer cared about the south; the east no longer cared about the west.

Greece was divided, which made it easier to conquer.

We must understand that the downfall of the Greek Empire reveals the downfall of a brass-level Christian. Regarding this downfall, the Bible says,

> "And that which fell among thorns are they, which, when they have heard, go forth, and are choked with cares and riches and pleasures of this life, and bring no fruit to perfection." Luke 8:14

Jesus using seeds as an example, revealed that some individuals could lose their salvation simply because they get carried away with the cares, riches, and pleasures of this life.

Christians who make up the brass stage genuinely want to be saved, but they want wealth a little more than they want salvation. Brass Christians desire to be righteous, but they are so caught up in the cares of this life that they may opt to wear the filthy rags of their own righteousness instead of putting on Christ's pure garments.

The life of a brass Christian is a series of ups and downs, or highs and lows. One day they can decide to give it all to Jesus, and the next day they may decide to take it all back. Their downfall comes because they have become so divided that their individual goals are beginning to outweigh the goals of the kingdom of heaven. Brass-level Christians are so divided between work, school, home, kids, spouse, and career that God often slips between the cracks.

It is okay to have worldly goals. There is nothing wrong with furthering careers. Being wealthy is not a sin, and the cares of this life should not be abandoned. The problem for brass-level Christians is that these cares become the focus of their lives, resulting in God taking a back seat. Brass-level Christians who are self-focused must be aware that they will fall to a new low if they continue down this path.

# Chapter 5

# **THE IRON PHASE**

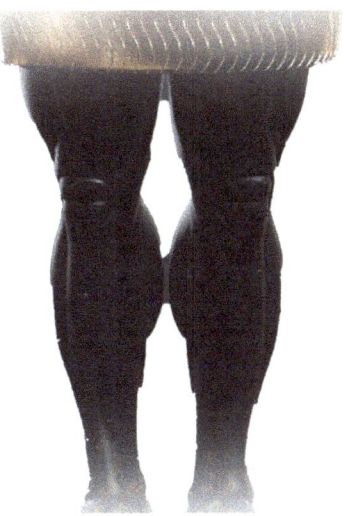

Believers who make up the iron phase of the image must know and understand where they are in relation to their soul salvation.

Iron-level Christians aren't really considered Christians. They are typically regarded as former Christians. What we must understand about this iron phase is that the individuals who make up this phase of the image have begun to separate from the church, which is proceeded by a separation from Christ. This separation may not be evident because iron-level Christians can still put on their church outfits and speak church lingo. Nevertheless, the characteristics of the iron phase should not be ignored.

Individuals who constitute the iron phase are only seen in church on one occasion...and that's called a special occasion. They will often put on their Sabbath best for Christmas, Easter, graduations, baby blessings, and funerals. This is typically the only time you will see an iron-phase believer in the sanctuary. If the planets align, you may be able to get them to attend a special day at your church, but unless they surrender their hearts to the call of the Spirit, they are typically there only to appease someone's request.

Iron-level believers see the value of the church because they were likely raised as Christian. Because they see this value, they may send their children to church schools and may even allow their child to attend church services, but do not expect an iron-phase individual to attend church with their child.

You may attempt to invite an iron-stage believer to an evangelistic effort or speak to them about the Sabbath truth, but the iron-phase believers are often well versed enough to maneuver their way out of most conversations with well-intentioned church members. Iron-stage believers will often disappoint family members who are still active in the church. However, what we must remember is that the iron phase is also the separation phase. The reason it's called the separation phase is because Satan blocks individuals from receiving the two components that are designed to keep members as a part of the church. The best way to explain these components is through my experience as a member of my local gym.

Working in Corporate America for the majority of my life has afforded me certain benefits. One of those benefits was having access to a gym on the campus of my workplace. Having the gym on campus gave me an opportunity to work out on a daily basis. I was diligent about exercising, and if I were placed on a lie detector, you would know that I was somewhat proud of my muscular physique. However, in 2018 my wife received a promotion for her job, and we decided, as a family, to move to a different city. Through the Lord's mercy, I was permitted to work remotely, which allowed me to keep my job. In order to maintain my muscular build, I purchased a used workout machine.

After a few months of working from home, I discovered that it was a struggle for me to work out. All I needed to do was simply open the door to the garage, and my gym was right there...but for some reason, I just couldn't do it. Why? Because there were two components that my campus gym had that my home gym lacked. Those two components are Community and Personal Accountability.

The gym that was located on campus provided each member with community. Community gave us a sense of belonging. I had many friends and coworkers who were also members of that gym; however, it wasn't until I moved that I realized how much of an impact their presence made on my desire to attend the gym. While working out at home had its benefits, sitting in a garage all by myself felt different.

The gym also provided each member with a sense of accountability. During my time at the campus gym, I obtained a few workout partners. On days that I really didn't feel like working out, I would ultimately still go to the gym just to avoid disappointing my workout partner. However, once I began working out in my home gym, there was no accountability. I lost motivation, and my muscular figure has since dissipated.

Satan realizes that the church often gives its members a sense of belonging (community) and is supposed to give its members responsibilities (accountability). If the community is friendly and inviting, and the members feel that there is equal accountability, they will often stay engaged in the church even when they are not living up to God's standard.

Iron-stage believers are more inclined to leave the church as their engagement with community and accountability deteriorate. Once the community and accountability are gone, iron believers become just like me—trying to work out in their garages.

The longer they are away from "campus," the harder it is for them to exercise true faith. Eventually, their Bibles collect dust, and religion no longer appeals to them. At this point, we must understand that even though individuals who make up the iron phase are losing the battle, Satan is not finished with their downfalls.

## The Downfall of the Iron Phase

Satan realized that the reason for Rome's downfall was the fact that it could not contain its borders. In other words, Rome's fall was due to an invasion.

What you must understand is that our eyes, ears, and mouths are like those Roman borders. We must guard them from Satanic influences. Unfortunately, iron-phase believers are more susceptible to Satanic possession than any of the previous levels of the image because they are no longer able to defend the "borders" of their soul.

Satan begins to rejoice in this stage because he realizes the borders of the iron believer's minds are wide open. At this leveling down in the iron stage, the believer's frontal lobes are wide open to Satan's suggestions. Truth becomes stranger than fiction, and wrong begins to look awfully right. Regarding this stage, the Bible says,

> "Woe unto them that call evil good, and good evil; that put darkness for light, and light for darkness; that put bitter for sweet, and sweet for bitter!" Isaiah 5:20

The borders of iron believer's eyes now become susceptible to Satanic illusions. Individuals in the iron stage can only see the faults of the church.

The borders of their ears are wide open, and they will begin listening to anything that sounds right.

# THE IRON PHASE • 53

Prior to this stage, believers could hear error and still discern that it was error; however, in this stage of the image, what was previously absurd now has validity; what could never be true might not be as farfetched as it once was. As Satan causes this downward move, iron believers will become extremely out of touch with reality.

The borders of their mouths are wide open, and they will begin acting as a mouthpiece for Satan. As Satan drags these individuals through the bottom stages of the iron, the invasion will begin speaking. All the things they were previously convicted of will suddenly become questionable. When they tell you that there are other ways to get to heaven outside of Jesus, please understand this is just the invasion speaking. When iron-stage believers tell you that there is no God, just know that this is the invasion speaking. It may even get to the point that they attempt to get others to leave the church along with them. When this happens, stand firm and know that the individual you are dealing with is on their way to the final stage of the image. Their deterioration is almost beyond repair.

# Chapter 6

# THE IRON AND CLAY PHASE

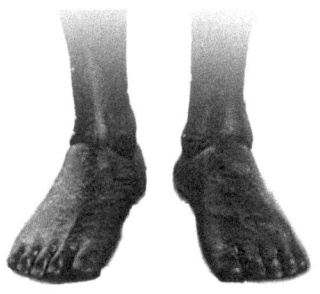

The iron and clay phase is the final stage of the image. Individuals in this stage will exhibit behavior that is nearly beyond repair. In case you are unaware, iron and clay individuals are essentially under the control of Satan. Some of the behavior exhibited by these individuals would be as follows:

Cynicism towards Christianity – When someone is cynical, it means they are skeptical, distrustful, or pessimistic. People in this phase will show contempt for the church and anything related to Christianity. Iron and clay individuals do not want your religion, nor do they want to hear about "your" God.

Anger towards Christianity - Individuals in the Iron and clay stage will often express anger towards God. Even if you are not trying to witness to them, they may still express anger towards you. They may even recall someone in the church that has hurt them or someone who wronged them and will use this as the motivation for their "crusade" against religion.

Whether they know it or not, individuals in the iron and clay phase exhibit the same tendencies as Papal Rome did during the Dark Ages—they are at war with God. Just like the Papal leaders tried to suppress the Word of God and persecute anyone who disagreed with them, the iron and clay stage consists of individuals who will attack anyone who has a desire to live by Christian principles. It matters not if you are a family, friend, or foe; if you are a believer in Christ, iron and clay individuals have you on their radar.

Individuals in this phase often bring sadness to their family and friends who are still in the church. What makes it worse is that iron and clay individuals cannot be reasoned with, which results in further frustration among their family and friends. It really feels like a no-win situation.

Whether they know it or not, individuals in this phase are preparing themselves for the final knockout punch from Satan. Yes, believe it or not, individuals in the early stages of the iron and clay can still come to Christ; all is not completely lost. However, you must also understand that Satan desires to get these individuals to the final stage of the image.

Remember, the final step in Nebuchadnezzar's dream was when a stone came and destroyed the image. In essence, what began as solid gold wound up as broken clay.

## The Downfall of the Iron and Clay Phase

The broken clay is the downfall of the iron and clay phase. Notice what the Bible says regarding individuals who reach this stage:

> "Wherefore I say unto you, All manner of sin and blasphemy shall be forgiven unto men: but the blasphemy against the Holy Ghost shall not be forgiven unto men. And whosoever speaketh a word against the Son of man, it shall be forgiven him: but whosoever speaketh against the Holy Ghost, it shall not be forgiven him, neither in this world,

> neither in the world to come." Matthew 12:31-32

> "And grieve not the holy Spirit of God, whereby ye are sealed unto the day of redemption." Ephesians 4:30

> "And even as they did not like to retain God in their knowledge, God gave them over to a reprobate mind, to do those things which are not convenient." Romans 1:28

Once individuals enter the broken clay phase, they have committed the unpardonable sin. In case you are unclear what the unpardonable sin is, let me define it:

The unpardonable sin is the point in someone's life that they no longer are able to hear the Holy Spirit. Don't be mistaken; there is no sin that is too difficult for God to forgive.... except the sin that is refused to be repented. The reason it is called the unpardonable sin is because individuals in this stage refuse to ask for forgiveness.

The unpardonable sin is like a spouse who continually cheats on his/her partner while refusing to acknowledge their indiscretions and ask for forgiveness. The offended spouse will soon realize that the cheating spouse cannot be forced to love him/her

# THE IRON AND CLAY PHASE • 59

and will often leave that individual to their own desires.

When someone has a reprobate mind, God does not force them to love Him. God realizes that this individual has put themselves in a place where they refuse to hear the voice of the Holy Spirit. If an individual refuses to hear the Holy Spirit's voice, then they essentially have no conscience. Once an individual has no conscience, they no longer can see their sinfulness.  An individual who cannot see their sinfulness cannot sense their need for a Savior and therefore refuses to take hold of God's saving grace. Now do you see why it's an unpardonable sin? This is why an individual who enters the broken clay phase is a lost soul.

If you are concerned that you have committed the unpardonable sin, you have not yet committed it. An individual in this phase is no longer concerned about their salvation. However, we must also be mindful that just because an individual has not committed the unpardonable sin does not mean they will be saved. This is why our wills must be wholly surrendered to Christ.

Now that we understand how the image relates to our salvation, we can see the step-by-step process that Satan uses to make a solid gold Christian a broken clay sinner:

1. **Pride** - You begin focusing on self-accomplishments.
2. **Underestimate Satan** – Because you are focused on your accomplishments, you underestimate Satan and begin to make small compromises with sin, leading to a major spiritual defeat.
3. **Focusing on self** – Your spiritual defeat causes you to focus more on self. Your worldly desires become your focus in life, and God gets pushed further and further out of your life.
4. **Acceptance of outside influences** – As the voice of God gets softer, Satan's voice gets louder. You become open to Satanic suggestions. Right seems wrong, and wrong seems right.
5. **Unpardonable sin** – As you become

> completely under the control of Satan, you grieve the Holy Spirit and declare war against the Word of God.

The steps are clearly outlined. This is how Satan can cause a believer to turn against all that he or she once believed.

As I contemplated these steps, it dawned on me that I was familiar with this process. As I reviewed the blueprint that Satan uses to get believers from solid gold to broken clay, I realized why Satan is so successful at deploying this scheme—the steps from solid gold to broken clay are the same steps Satan experienced in his transition from Lucifer to Satan.

## Lucifer's solid gold to broken clay experience

> ### Gold
> "Thou wast perfect in thy ways from the day that thou wast created..." Ezekiel 28:15

In the beginning, Lucifer was created as a perfect being. Like all the other angels, he delighted in listening to the voice of God and following His commands. It should be clear that Lucifer was in the golden phase. However, we must remember that there is one downfall to those who are in the gold phase—

they develop pride. Notice what the Bible says about Lucifer's downward slide from the gold phase:

> "Thine heart was lifted up because of thy beauty ..." Ezekiel 28:17

Are you seeing this? Lucifer was created in the gold phase; however, just like Babylon, he began focusing on himself. Regarding this self-exaltation, Ellen White states the following:

> "Little by little, Lucifer came to indulge the desire for self-exaltation.... Though all his glory was from God, this mighty angel came to regard it as pertaining to himself." *Patriarchs and Prophets, p. 35*

> "... he began to seek his own honor, and to employ his powers to attract attention and win praise to himself." *The Spirit of Prophecy Vol 4, p. 317*

This prideful spirit is what caused Lucifer to transition from gold to silver.

### Silver

As Lucifer continued to develop the spirit of pride, his transition to silver caused him to overestimate himself and underestimate God. On this point, the Bible says,

> "...thou hast corrupted thy wisdom by reason of thy brightness..." Ezekiel 28:17

On this point, Ellen White's commentary says,

> "His heart was filled with love and joy in serving his Creator, until he began to think that his wisdom was not derived from God, but was inherent in himself, and that he was as worthy as was God to receive honor and power." *The Signs of the Times, September 18, 1893*

Lucifer began to believe that he was the reason for his exalted position in heaven. He began to overestimate himself and underestimate God. What he didn't know was that these small compromises would soon lead to a major fall.

### Brass

Lucifer began focusing more on himself and less on his Creator. As the purposes of God became less of a concern, Lucifer's priorities shifted to his own aspirations. Regarding his aspirations, the Bible says,

> "For thou hast said in thine heart, I will ascend into heaven, I will exalt my throne above the stars of God: I will sit also upon the mount of the

> congregation, in the sides of the north."
> Isaiah 14:13

Whether he knew it or not, Lucifer was moving further and further away from God.

### Iron

As Lucifer got further and further from God, wrong started feeling right, and right began to appear wrong. It was at this point that Lucifer allowed his thoughts to overtake him, and the seed of evil began to sprout. The Bible gives us evidence of this moment when it says,

> "...till iniquity was found in thee."
> Ezekiel 28:15

Once iniquity was found in him, he ceased to be Lucifer. Thus, the transition to the one whom we call the Devil, the Dragon, or Satan was complete.

### Iron and Clay

In this stage, Satan, declared war against God Himself. Regarding this declaration, the Bible says,

> "And there was war in heaven: Michael and his angels fought against the dragon; and the dragon fought and his angels." Revelation 12:7

# THE IRON AND CLAY PHASE • 65

All hope for Lucifer was lost. God removed Satan and the angels that rebelled with him. The Bible reveals this supernatural eviction:

> "And the great dragon was cast out, that old serpent, called the Devil, and Satan, which deceiveth the whole world: he was cast out into the earth, and his angels were cast out with him."
> Revelation 12:9

Once Satan was kicked out of heaven, the image was complete—Satan transitioned from solid gold to broken clay.

Satan has taken this process, refined it, perfected it, and utilizes it masterfully against every person who has claimed the name of Christ.

So now that we understand the steps of Nebuchadnezzar's image, we must ask ourselves— Does God have an antidote for Satan's blueprint? After searching the Scriptures, I realized one of my favorite verses outlines how we can combat Satan's blueprint. Yes, there is a solution! The Bible reveals how we can get back to gold!

## Chapter 7

# GETTING BACK TO GOLD

Many of you reading this book already know what phase of the image you currently belong. Wherever you are in relation to the image, I need you to know that God is still in the saving business. You may be reading this book realizing that you have left the gold or possibly are deep into the brass stage. Some of you may even come to the realization that you are in the vicinity of the broken clay. Wherever you are, my message to you is that God has not left you without the blueprint to get back to gold.

As I reviewed the stages of the image, I realized that one of the most quoted scriptures is also the antidote for the fall from gold to broken clay. Notice the scripture that God has given us to combat this spiritual deterioration:

> "If my people, which are called by my name, shall humble themselves, and pray, and seek my face, and turn from their wicked ways; then will I hear from heaven, and will forgive their sin, and will heal their land." 2Chronicles 7:14

Whether you know it or not, hidden within this text is the formula to reverse Satan's design to take us from solid gold to broken clay. If you look closely, 2Chronicles 7:14 can be divided into four parts:

1. Humble yourself
2. Pray
3. Seek God's face
4. Turn from your wicked ways

If you are in danger of falling from gold to silver, the scripture is clear. You must **HUMBLE YOURSELF**. While you are likely doing a great work for the Lord, you must also understand that this work is because of the power of God in you. You must remember that the spirit of pride is what caused Lucifer to fall from heaven. If pride can cause Lucifer to fall while in the direct presence of God, what makes you believe you can stand while living on this sinful earth without Him?

Whenever you receive a complement, you must

resist the urge to entertain any prideful thoughts. You must ask God for help so that you can fight any thoughts that may cause you to believe that you are the reason for your success. Yes, you may be a great preacher, teacher, singer, or author, but never forget that God is the source of all your success.

If you are in the silver phase, you are starting to take "small" defeats in your walk with Christ. You see these small compromises, but you are not sure what you can do to reverse your situation. The scripture is clear—you must **PRAY**. Almost every relationship that is going sour will have one commonality—little to no communication. Considering that Jesus took the time to pray and commune with His Father is all the motivation we need. Follow God's Word and pray without ceasing.

If you are in the brass phase, you are starting to seek your own agenda over God's agenda. The cares of this life are overtaking the cares of the next life. You may be focusing on your family, or your career, or just trying to live life. There is no shame in taking care of anything I just mentioned. As a matter of fact, to neglect these things can also be displeasing to God. However, you must have balance. The scripture says you must **SEEK GOD'S FACE!** Right now, you may be seeking the face of everything around you except the face of God. Just like a neglected spouse who wants to be pursued, God wants you to seek His face! This means you must spend more time with God. This can be through prayer, singing hymns, Bible study, or even witnessing. Whatever method the Spirit of God reveals to you, you must follow and seek His face.

If you are in the iron or the iron and clay phase, you may be fighting demonic influences. Even worse, you may be fighting against God Himself. You may feel like your life is slipping away, but let me reveal to you that God specializes in people who feel like they are slipping away from Him. God has one request for you—**TURN FROM YOUR WICKED WAYS**. Whatever you are doing, if you ask, God will give you the power to resist. God has not given up on you, and he will help you not give up on Him. Turn from your wicked ways, start seeking His face, pray as much as you can, and remain humble.

It should be clear, the only person whom God cannot save is the individual who refuses to be saved. God could force everyone to go to heaven, but he has given us the power of choice. If you chose Christ today, He will choose you on that great day.

> "While it is said, To day if ye will hear his voice, harden not your hearts..." Hebrews 3:15

# FROM SOLID GOLD TO BROKEN CLAY
A CLEAR AND PRESENT TRUTH MESSAGE

www.ingramcontent.com/pod-product-compliance
Lightning Source LLC
Chambersburg PA
CBHW062153100526
44589CB00014B/1811